TAX WITHOUT TEARS

Tax and accounts for the
self-employed and those
working from home....

Robert Sherwood

Published by
Filament Publishing
14, Croydon Road, Waddon
Croydon, Surrey CR0 4PA
Telephone +44 (0)20 8688 2598
info@filamentpublishing.com
www.filamentpublishing.com

© 2011 Robert Sherwood
Fourth Edition

ISBN 978-1-905493-29-6

Printed by Antony Rowe, Eastbourne

DSL Accounting.
Botanical House, 15 Guy's Cliffe Road,
Leamington Spa Warwickshire CV32 5BZ
Tel: 01926 422872 Fax: 01926 435211
www.dslaccounting.co.uk

Foreword

As Direct Selling is now the UK's largest provider of independent earning opportunities, it has become increasingly important that every direct seller gets the right help to run a proper business of their own.

A simple, tailor-made, and easy to understand book on accounting for direct sellers to use was long overdue, and that is what Robert Sherwood has written. The book has our full support.

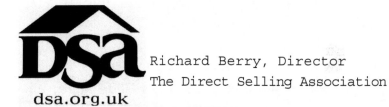

Richard Berry, Director
The Direct Selling Association

dsa.org.uk

Staying up to date

To keep you up to date with the latest
tax rates and key dates for this year,
and for free downloads of useful forms and tables,
go to our website,

www.dslaccounting.co.uk

For personal advice on all tax matters
contact us at

DSL Accounting Ltd.
Botanical House, 15 Guy's Cliffe Road,
Leamington Spa
Warwickshire CV32 5BZ
Tel: 01926 422872
Fax: 01926 435211
www.dslaccounting.co.uk

Table of Contents

Starting up as self-employed

and don't know what to do?

Find out everything you need to know!

Chapter 1

Introduction

This book is written for all those people who are both self-employed and work from home. There are now many such businesses including direct selling, therapies of many kinds, consultancies, franchising, fashion and the arts, sports trainers, all sorts of services and even small manufacturers. Some sell their products or services using traditional methods, others by party plan or person to person, and many using the Internet or through EBay. Their records, books of account and annual returns follow much the same pattern and include many common categories of income and expenditure.

This book is aimed at the person who is looking for help and advice in setting up in business and maintaining a system of records which will achieve a number of different goals:

- Keep track of financial accounts
- Provide the necessary figures for tax and VAT returns
- Create a routine allowing more time for the actual business

- Give peace of mind knowing that all accounting functions are in place

I have written this book from a dual standpoint. First of all I qualified as a Chartered Accountant many years ago and so I fully understand the requirements of Her Majesty's Revenue & Customs (HMRC), and secondly I have been involved with the direct selling industry for the past 15 years, first as a successful distributor and since 1997 running an accountancy practice specialising in helping direct sellers cope with tax and accounting issues. I now want to use this experience to support the rest of the self-employed market along similar lines.

Chapter 2

The Importance of Keeping Accounts

I set out in this chapter 5 different reasons for keeping accounts and why they should form an integral part of your business and not just be a necessary evil.

1. Particularly in the early days of a new business, it is important to watch the level of expenditure and not let it get out of control. It's a good idea before you start to prepare a simple budget on what you can afford to spend in the first 6-12 months before income starts to kick in and sales begin to generate cash flow. Regular accounting will tell you how your expenses are running compared with your budget, and will also enable you to compare monthly income against monthly expenditure.

2. Talking of expenditure, the cost of an accountant to prepare your annual accounts and tax return is usually based on the time it takes to do the work. For most accountants time equals money, so if you can reduce time by doing much of the work yourself, you will reduce the fee. In other words if you do all the basic bookkeeping and present to

Keep your accounts

up to date and then you will be able to

see how your

business is progressing!

an accountant simply an annual summary asking just for your tax return to be completed, you will have saved your accountant a lot of time and yourself a lot of money. On the other hand if you hand over a pile of papers with a week to go before the deadline date, don't blame the accountant for charging a large fee - remember you could have done much more yourself.

3. Being self-employed and working from home gives rise to lots of opportunities for claiming legitimate expenses for tax purposes, and many of these are simply converting a domestic cost into a tax allowable claim.

'Private' costs are in many cases now classed as 'business' and as such will impact strongly on levels of profit and tax payable. However, without a proper set of account and records, such expenses cannot readily be quantified and certainly cannot be easily substantiated if required at a later date.

4. Many self-employed people start off part-time retaining their previous employment until such time as the new cash flow matches the old, and as part of this process the set up and running costs of the new venture will initially and inevitably

"If this carries on we're going to lose all our tax losses."

exceed income. We call this a 'tax loss' and under current UK tax regulations, during the first four years of a new business, this can be offset against taxed income (e.g. salary or pension) and some of the PAYE recovered. This can be applied on a same year basis, or in cases where employment no longer applies, you can backdate a claim for up to 3 years. This is a great way of covering part of your initial investment but, of course, without any accurate accounts you cannot quantify the 'tax loss' and thereby you'll miss out on the tax refund.

5. From time to time there will arise the need to borrow money. It may be a new mortgage or funds for the business, but in every case the lender will want to know the levels of income and profit to support the loan. No accounts = no evidence = no loan!

"STEVE, I ADMIRE YOUR DETERMINATION TO MAKE THIS PLAN WORK."

Chapter 3

Business Plan

There are 2 main categories of business plans, one directed towards raising finance and the other more of a strategic planning exercise. The well known maxim that "failing to plan is planning to fail" applies to both of them. This chapter looks at the finance based plan.

Raising finance might be restricted to a particular area, buying business vehicles, equipment, etc., when a fully blown plan is unlikely to be required - then it's more a case of valuing the asset to be acquired, supplying a bank reference and maybe a personal guarantee. I am more concerned with a typical business start up which requires working capital and ongoing funding first to create and then to nurture a new venture until it reaches a self-financing stage. Before considering the actual contents of a plan, let's consider what is its purpose.

I have identified a number of 'purposes' which need to be borne in mind when drafting a planning document. In the first place you will be seeking to give comfort to the lender or investor so as to

If you fail to plan....

you are planning to fail.

Don't let this happen to you!

justify the financial risk they are taking. Everything you include in the plan should be aimed at convincing the lender/investor that both you and your project are likely to succeed and provide a good return. Secondly, by putting together such a plan, you yourself will be focussing your own mind onto your business finances, and visualising what is needed to create a successful enterprise. At the same time you will be building up a model which can later be used to plot actual progress against the planned or budgeted version - an essential exercise as time goes on - and then finally you should aim to convince a lender/investor that you are building a business not just for the immediate term or the period of a loan, but one which has a much longer life span - more a case of wanting to back <u>you</u>, than just one particular project.

Now let's put you into the shoes of a lender for a few minutes and ask what would you be looking to find in a prospective borrower - here are a few questions you'd probably ask:

- What track record in business does the borrower have?

- Is the business itself sound?

Encourage the reader to

want to see more

- How established is the company behind it?

- Is there any security for a loan?

- Is the borrower of reliable character?

- Can the business support a repayment programme? Over how long?

- Is the borrower capable of running a profitable business?

- What other support than just finance will be required?

OK, I've set the scene now, so let's concentrate on the actual content of the business plan. I think there should be 6 sections as follows:

- An Introduction

- The Background

- The Market

- Management

- Future Plans

- Finance

Be in good shape to convince a lender that you are able to support a loan

We'll go through each in turn.

The first section, Introduction, is setting the scene and trying to entice the reader to want to move on and look through the more detailed analysis. This section will quantify the financial requirement and briefly tell the lender/investor what the business plan is all about, inviting him or her to look further. Also the wider picture of how the product or service would fit into the type of industry or business sector concerned is part of the introduction. It is all about wetting the appetite, interesting the reader and giving a positive impression about the project.

The second section, Background to the project, is used to explain the history of the business to date or, if brand new, a record of comparable businesses so far, give a description of the product or service being offered and the various sources of income involved - for example in a direct selling business you would describe how earnings come from retail sales, and how also you can earn commission in a variety of different ways from recruiting others to carry out similar functions to yourself. Then, not just with the income in mind, describe how the business will actually operate, the premises required, any manufacturing process,

Notes Page

and, very importantly, any patents, copyright or similar 'intangible asset value' owned. If you ever watch "Dragons' Den" you'll have noticed how importantly the panel rates the ownership of exclusive rights to a product or process.

Now let's turn to the Market in which the business is going to operate and how it will reach its potential customers. These might be retail customers resulting from an advertising campaign, customers driven to a website from a search engine, customers arriving by trading out of a prime location and many more opportunities. Describe the selling techniques that best suit your business, the costs involved and the expected numbers you are targeting. Go into any sales or marketing methods available to you including taking on sales staff, telemarketing, traditional advertising and the Internet. Describe the customer profile and explain why they should become <u>your</u> customer; what are you offering or providing better than anyone else?

Explain how your particular market might expand or how you have found a perfect niche in which to operate. What does the future hold? How can you expand your customer base or, if you supply one particular customer the majority of your product, how secure is this? Do you have a contract?

Notes Page

Give the investor reasons to think that you have covered all sales and marketing opportunities, and at the same time have taken prudent steps to protect your business.

The section on Management is to let the lender/investor assess your own business acumen and whether you are likely, based on your past history, to succeed. Give a brief and relevant synopsis of your business career to date, the experience you have, and appropriate qualifications. Do a similar exercise on any key players in your business or describe the kind of people you will be looking to recruit. In certain cases you might be looking for an investor to play a hands-on role in your business but be careful how you play this - it should not be seen as an existing gap and thereby a weak point.

As to the Future, investors often look beyond the immediate project so you should paint the picture of where the business can go - banks like this too; a customer for life, not just a project. Obviously be reasonable in your forecasting, make the future realistic but at the same time make it long term and promising. If relevant, mention future markets, moving from local to national or even to an international customer base. Put some timing

Make sure you get

10 out of 10 for presentation!

predictions into growth, again realistic, but mindful also that investors like to back successful entrepreneurs who are ambitious.

Every backer of every project will quickly home in to the Financial forecasting, and again if you watch "Dragons' Den" you'll have seen that if you don't get your figures right you are soon sent back down the stairs! What do you need? If it's an existing business you'll need figures from the past, turnover, direct costs and net profit, being the most important ones. A balance sheet or statement of affairs at a current date is also vital - no lender/investor wants to finance existing liabilities unless they really have to - so you want to show a nice clean start position.

If, of course, it has no previous history, the cash flow and profits forecasts become all important. These are designed to show over say a 12 month period how the business will function, the level of sales/cash coming in compared with costs, overheads, loan repayments and so on. By setting out a typical cash flow forecast you can plot on a monthly basis the moving balance and judge how much extra finance will be required to sustain the business. An interesting and absolutely unavoidable exercise, and you may well need help in preparing it.

Strengths

Threats SWOT Weaknesses

Opportunities

It must be realistic because if the actual figures soon differ widely from those forecasted trouble is brewing! Better by far to exceed your forecast, so realism is much more important than optimism at this early stage. See sample Cashflow Projection on pages 87-89.

Finally, a few words on presentation. As virtually no lending or investing is done nowadays without a business plan, make yours really stand out. A nice neat layout is essential, you are trying to impress! Attach any relevant industry or marketing material including photographs or design images, if relevant, and don't worry about one section overlapping into another - this is inevitable and only serves to emphasise a particular point.

You may have heard of a SWOT exercise - this stands for Strengths, Weaknesses, Opportunities and Threats - and is a useful addition to a plan because it shows you have properly considered both your positive position and its potential problem areas.

- Strengths might include existing available finance, uniqueness and patents already in place

Do your own S.W.O.T analysis here

- Weaknesses could be a 'one-man band' and no previous marketing skills

- Opportunities might be potential follow-up products and new markets

- Threats could include cheap foreign competition

Do a few of your own and hopefully the balance will come out on the positive side - if not, maybe you should think again or at least take positive steps to redress the balance.

Notes Page

Chapter 4

Setting up in Business

Quite apart from the logistics of acquiring stock, creating an office at home and doing all the practical things that a new business requires, there are a couple of tax and accounting issues to address.

First of all you will probably need to register as self-employed with the Inland Revenue, now known as HMRC. I say "probably" because this is not necessary if you are already registered as self-employed and have your 'UTR', Unique Tax Reference, a 10 digit number used on all HMRC returns and statements. If you intend to work with a partner, then the same situation applies, both of you must register if not already in place.

Registration is simply a form filling exercise, forms CWF1 and CF10 for a sole trader, or SA400 and SA401 for a partnership. You will see in CF10 at box 12 you need to enter the expected first year's profits, and if these are below £5,075 in 2009/10 or £5,315 in 2011/12 then you can choose not to pay self-employed NI contributions. At the same time this exception also prevents HMRC from charging a £100 late filing penalty otherwise due if these

**You must register as
self-employed with HMRC**

forms are filed more that three months after the declared start date. Under current legislation you can afford to file late provided the CF10 is filed along with the CWF1, and declares an expected profit below the threshold, and in your first period of trading this is very likely to be true anyway. However, legislation is a moveable feast, so be sure to avoid a penalty, filing on time is advisable.

It's always best to get this process over as soon as possible and then your UTR will follow enabling you to file your tax return on time - remember you can't submit a tax return without this official reference number. More on tax returns later.

If you decide that you want to start paying self -employed NI contributions voluntarily from the word go, then you will need to complete a direct debit form, and the weekly contributions will be collected on a monthly basis. The weekly rate for both 2009/10 and 2010/11 is £2.40, but rising to £2.50 in 2011/12.

Registration sets you up officially in business, and of course from the chosen start date you can begin to claim all the expenses incurred which I will describe later. There's now one more step to take as soon as practicable, and this is to arrange for a

**Make life easier -
use a bank account
and credit card solely
for your business**

new bank account. Ideally this is available from the start, although many people simply use their existing personal account for the new business too. I don't recommend this for 3 reasons.

Firstly it'll make accounting a much messier exercise having to extract business items from personal ones.

Secondly any personal account bank charges or interest could not be fully claimed for tax purposes being partially due to private expenditure, and thirdly if ever HMRC ask to see your business bank statements as part of a routine enquiry, you'll be showing them personal items too - and you might not want to!

As soon as possible, therefore, ask your bank for a separate account and the same goes for a credit card too - try to use one card exclusively for business purposes, and life will be a lot easier. One exercise you'll need to do regularly is to go through both your bank and credit card accounts and pick out direct debits, standing orders and charges so you can record them in your accounting system. It's far easier to do this when you know that all entries in the bank or credit card statements refer only to your business.

Keep your accounting

records on track

and everyone will be happy!

Chapter 5

Records

HMRC do not lay down a prescribed form of records. The only requirement is that all receipts and payments are so recorded that the end result for an accounting year (or shorter period) accurately reflects the profit or loss. It is also a requirement that all bills and receipts are retained for a period of 6 years, and by implication these should be referenced and filed in such a way that an easy trace can be followed if a particular bill needs to be located from the accounting records.

Think of the accounts as a trail of paperwork, starting with each individual receipt and ending as a tax or VAT return. In between will be daily figures, monthly summaries and annual accounts.

Self-employed accounts can be prepared on either a 'cash' or an 'accruals' basis. Cash means recording income or expenditure at the time it is actually received or paid, whereas accruals required entries to be made on the date that sales invoices are raised or purchase invoices received. Accounts can be on a simple income and expenditure basis with no need also to prepare a balance sheet unless, of course

Notes Page

your business is being run as a limited company, where the regulations are quite different and full accounts are obligatory.

There should be a bill or receipt for each receipt or payment, but if after trying to obtain one this is not possible, then make one out yourself regarding its date and nature. If you are VAT registered (see later), each payment must be supported by a VAT receipt, so when using your credit card for example, you must obtain a separate receipt showing the suppliers VAT registration number as the credit card slip will not. When you make sales, each invoice must show your VAT number and the VAT charged, and all invoices should be sequentially numbered.

If you are given bills by suppliers which do not show the VAT element separately based on a VAT rate of 17.5% you can calculate this by using the fraction 7/47, or at 15% as now, 3/23. From 4th January 2011 when VAT rises to 20%, the fraction will then be 1/6.

Filing paperwork is best done on a monthly basis, continuing a numeric sequence from month to month. Simply write in the top right hand corner of the invoice the respective number, record the reference in your accounting records and years later you should have no problem finding it!

Notes Page

Retail sales are often recorded individually in duplicate receipt books, but if for example you are holding a home party generating multiple sales, you could group these together as one item in your accounting records - the individual receipts are retained in the duplicate book for future reference.

Split your income into the different categories applicable to your type of business and see where your strengths lie!

Chapter 6

Income

Receipts into a business will vary according to how it operates, but broadly can be divided amongst the following categories:

- Retail Sales

- Wholesale Sales

- Fees

- Commission

- Rent Received

- Interest Received

In addition you would need to include a miscellaneous category as there is certain to be receipts which don't easily fall into one of those above.

One source of receipt which will not be classed as income is any capital introduced by the proprietor or partner in the business. You'll obviously need to record these amounts particularly in the case of a

Notes Page

partnership, but they will not form any part of the 'trading income' of the business and will not be part of any taxable profit. Capital introduced may be initial capital injected to set up the business, or any amounts of ongoing investment to be used as working capital. In addition a VAT or tax refund would be classed as further capital introduced. The accumulated total is always a key figure when applying for third party loans as it reflects your own commitment to your business - if you don't invest in your own firm why should anyone else?

Retail Sales -   These are sales of goods or services to your retail customers, either singly or aggregated as previously described.

Wholesale Sales -   These are sales to any wholesale customers or in the case of a direct selling business to your downline distributors.

Fees -   These are 'Retail Sales' too, but in a professional practice would normally be termed 'Fees'. The implication is

Notes Page

that of providing a service rather that selling products.

Commission -   This form of income usually comes by way of rewarding the recipient for achieving targets and introducing new business, or can simply be based on a percentage of turnover. In a direct selling company it will also be known as royalties or bonuses and is always performance based. Other businesses likely to receive commission income are sales agencies, insurance brokers or property based professionals.

Rent Received -   This is where the business as opposed to its owner(s) receives rental income, maybe because it is a letting business or because it sublets part of its premises if it is not entirely home based.

Notes Page

Interest Received - This can come from bank deposit interest, late payments by customers or from any business loans made from surplus funds.

In times of the 'squeeze' are you claiming everything you are entitled to?

Chapter 7

Expenditure

There will be many categories of expenses common to all businesses, particularly amongst the overheads, so let me first list all the various possible headings then go into further detail where necessary. Of course not all categories will apply in some cases.

Cost of Sales

1. These are what is known as the "direct costs", i.e. those which impact directly on sales

2. Products costs adjusted annually for opening and closing stock

3. Discounts given to customers or royalties paid to franchisors

4. Samples and demonstration goods given away with no price attached

5. Consumable items, i.e. small parts, tools, cleaning materials and any costs involved with manufacture or assembly

6.   Packaging

7.   Transport and delivery charges including any import duty

Overheads

These are the running costs of a business.

1. Personnel - Labour related costs

- Salaries or wages, but not personal drawings

- Casual labour, including family members

- Training & courses

2. Premises - Either home-based or for separate business premises

- Rent

- Council tax

- Utilities

- Insurance

- Repairs & renewals

3. Travel

- Motor expenses or mileage claim

- Other travel costs, home & overseas conferences, etc.

- Subsistence & hotel bills

- Entertaining

- Car leasing or contract hire

4. Administration

- Telephone, fax & Internet charges

- Post & stationery

- Computer costs, but not purchase of equipment

- Printing of letterheads, business cards, etc.

- Legal & professional charges, including accountancy

5. Selling

- Advertising

- Promotion, including books, tapes, brochures, etc.

- Exhibitions

- Incentives, gifts, introductory fees & commission

- Bad debts

- Samples & demonstration products given away

6. Finance

- Bank charges

- Bank interest

- Credit card charges

- Hire purchase interest & finance charges

7. Capital Expenditure

- Costs of vehicles

- Costs of office equipment, computers & furniture

- The capital element of HP & finance instalments

8. Drawings

This category is not claimable as a business expense but needs to be recorded.

See notes on 'Capital Introduced' in the income section.

- Personal drawings of cash

- Personal costs paid for by the business

- National insurance contributions

- Tax and VAT payments

Notes Page

Further Comments

Cost of Sales

1 & 4

A number of businesses will not be selling products, e.g. telecom companies dealing with airtime, but for those who do there will be products for selling on to customers, and also products to give away as samples. Having split the figure appropriately, you can elect to transfer the cost of samples and demo stock to selling expenses, category 5.

You should also evaluate the stock of products at the end of each year at cost prices, and adjust the cost of products bought <u>during</u> the year by adding the opening stock and subtracting the closing figure. This gives a more accurate 'usage' figure for the accounts.

Overheads

1. Personnel

When claiming for family members it is important actually to make such payments, and to record them. Also in the case of claiming for children make sure they are capable and old enough to carry out any duties you are claiming they perform.

Notes Page

2. Premises

This section gives you a legal opportunity to convert private expenses into tax deductible claims. Base your 'office at home' claims by excluding rooms where no work is possible, i.e. kitchen, bathroom and loos, and then claiming a fraction of costs equal to the number of remaining bedrooms and reception rooms - e.g. 3 bedrooms, 1 lounge and 1 dining room equals 5 - so claim 1/5.

I don't recommend adding mortgage interest to the list as this might cause a capital gains tax charge to be levied when selling your home at a profit, and for the same reason never claim that a room is exclusively used as an office, always maintain a secondary use, e.g. a spare bedroom for occasional use.

3. Travel

The tax treatment of entertainment by HMRC is usually to disallow it despite the fact that often it is both necessary and very much part of business. This probably is a case where commercial advantage outweighs the loss of any tax allowance.

Subsistence should be allowed but there is a level of inconsistency within different tax districts.

What certainly helps is if your claims are based around official meetings set up for example to discuss sales with your customers, training with your organisation or new product launches with your company. Claims for accommodation, meals, etc., in these circumstances are much more likely to succeed. Taking a few friends down to the pub or out to a restaurant and talking business will not find a sympathetic Tax Inspector's ear.

Whether to base motor expenses on bills and receipts or a mileage claim is another question. For both you'll need mileage records for in the case of bills and receipts (plus in this case a capital allowance on the actual vehicle) you need to determine the appropriate % to use, based on business miles against total miles.

For a mileage claim after 6 April 2011 you can claim 45p for the first 10,000 miles and 25p thereafter. Previous to this the first 10,000 miles could be claimed at 40p. In addition you can claim an extra 5p per passenger on a business journey.

This applies to both self-employment and employment...you don't aggregate miles and thereby reduce the claim, each situation is calculated in full.

New rules came into effect on 6th April 2009 and for vehicles bought after that date claims are based on CO_2 emissions. Prior to 6th April 2009, there is a special tax treatment for contract hire on cars with a value exceeding £12,000, which reduces the claim from the actual cost to an amount based on this formula

$$\text{Annual Charge} \times \frac{£12,000 + \text{Retail Value}}{2 \times \text{Retail Value}}$$

The new basis states that if emissions exceeds 160 g/km, then 15% of the expenditure is disallowed.

4. Administration

For telephone claims where there will be private use, an appropriate % needs to be used; this can be based on an examination of a sample month's bill, but as dedicated business lines are introduced, these qualify for a 100% claim.

5. Selling

HMRC often don't appreciate the need to give flowers, bottles of champagne, etc., as rewards to people who have helped your business. The important thing to point out is that in most cases it is a reward for having achieved something, rather than an incentive to do so in the future. That makes the claim easier to justify. 'Finder's fees' can certainly be claimed if appropriate.

The question is are you

a sole trader,

in a partnership

or a limited company?

Chapter 8

Annual Accounts

The purpose of this chapter is to consider what 'Annual Accounts' should comprise, are there any legal requirements, and for whom they are intended. The answers to these questions largely depends on whether you are trading as self-employed, in a partnership or as a limited company..... there are major differences in the level of reporting between these 3 categories..... let's take them in turn but first there is another issue to consider which will affect all of them.

Accounts can be prepared on a 'cash' basis or an 'accruals' basis. This means that you can either adopt a method of only recording a transaction when it is either an actual payment or receipt, or base your accounting system on receiving invoices for expenditure and issuing invoices for income. In the latter case life is more complicated as you have also to account in a separate way for payments or receipts which frequently will follow the invoices later on. It is customary, and very sensible too, for a relatively small business to adopt the cash basis whereas a Limited Company has to work on the accruals system.

Notes Page

Now let's look at what annual accounts should include and treat each category in turn:

Self-employed traders really only need an income and expenditure or profit and loss account. A balance sheet which records year end balances and reflects 'the state of play' at a particular date is not a legal requirement, and if provided to the HMRC within a tax return often leads to more questions!

Just base your accounts on what you have paid and what you have received within a chosen accounting period. The only 2 adjustments to make for tax purposes are firstly for any private element of an expense item, telephone for example or motor expenses, where you have probably entered all monies paid out in either case, although both costs include private use. For tax purposes you need to reduce the claim by an appropriate proportion.

The second adjustment needed is to add any trading stock held at the beginning of an accounting period to the purchase of products, and then deduct similar stock held at the end. This is designed so as to reflect more accurately the actual usage of stock during the period. Apart from these 2 areas, everything in the sole trader's accounts should be on a cash basis, and don't worry about a balance sheet,

Working as a partnership might necessitate a period end balance sheet in order to reflect the respective 'capital accounts' of the partners. By this I mean that from time to time one or more partners might bring in money to the business, take money out, or enjoy a different profit share. In case the business is later sold, or a partner retires, these 'capital accounts' are important accounting issues, unless you are talking about a husband and wife situation where such considerations would not normally arise... except in a divorce of course! Apart from this consideration, the accounts could follow the sole trader format.

It is with a Limited Company that legal requirements arise and certain accounting principles apply. These accounts must be prepared on an accrual basis with a balance sheet that shows debtors – sales invoices not yet paid by the customer – and creditors – expenditure of all kinds for which an invoice has been received but not yet paid, plus any taxes or other liabilities due at that date. Accounting in this way is obviously a more extensive exercise than purely cash accounting. The balance sheet must also include the cost of any fixed assets, that is cars and equipment, computers and so on, together with the accumulated depreciation charge, and value of trading stock, the bank and cash balances and, if relevant, any hire purchase instalments still outstanding.

In other words it is a statement of the company's position at a certain date and having listed the items above, they should be matched by what is known as 'capital & reserves', that is the amount of share capital contributed from time to time by shareholders and the accumulated profits and losses of the business since the beginning. The balance sheet is designed to show how funds raised through share capital and profits have been allocated or spent over the years.

If this sounds complicated, you can well understand why it is best left to Limited Companies, which have to report in this way, and only prepare profit and loss accounts for sole traders. Partnerships which are not 'all family' affairs sit in the middle, no obligation for a balance sheet but sometimes desirable.

Year end accounts may have to serve two purposes, they will certainly be required to give the figures to enter into either the sole trader or

Notes Page

partnership tax returns – only in the case of a Limited Company are the actual accounts submitted at the initial stage – but accounts will also be needed when borrowing is required either for business purposes or maybe to support a mortgage application. Obviously low profits mean less tax, but they also might negate a mortgage application ... sadly there is little you can do about this ... you can't have 2 sets of figures ... this is not Italy!!

The final issue is choosing an accounting date. For Limited Companies it does not matter, as tax is due 9 months and one day after the year end and accounts have to be filed at Companies House 10 months after the year end. For sole traders and partnerships 31st March is the easiest as it coincides with the tax year. This might mean an initial period of less than 12 months but this accelerates any tax refund following a 'tax loss' as described in Chapter 2, (4).

Self-assessment supplement -

find out what goes where

Chapter 9

Tax Returns

The self-assessment tax return comprises a main body and several separate parts, depending from where your income arrives. In this book I am only dealing with the self-employed supplement which will record the details of your business annual or periodic accounts. The accounts themselves do not go to the Tax Inspector, only an actual return. If you start your business part way through a tax year, close off your accounts at the following 31st March (you need not actually go to 5th April), and then start again from 1st April. Your first accounts in this case will therefore be for less than a year, but it is easier to follow the tax year from then on rather than sticking to the anniversary of your actual start date. This also brings forward the receipt of any initial tax repayment.

Current tax returns incorporate a layout including a section for self-employed income, but partnerships still use the old format. This will surely change soon.

Self-employment is divided into a "short" or a "full" version. "Short" means that turnover (in direct selling this means commission plus personal - not group - sales) is less than £67,000 p.a., and again in this section if turnover is less than £30,000 no expenses details are required, only the total allowable expenses figure is entered. Otherwise in both the short and full versions there are various boxes in which to enter the figures for categories of expense - more detail in the full version.

Elsewhere in this form, you will record the address of your business (home in most cases), the nature of your work and the period of the accounts.

I mentioned earlier that the cost of cars or computers, etc., are treated differently from other expenses. You will find a separate section to record the 'capital allowance' on these, which is then shown separately. New rules which came in on 6th April 2009 change the calculation basis. Up until then you apply 20% to the cost during the year, or 20% of the written down value brought forwards from the previous year, i.e.

Cost in year 1	10,000
1st year - 20% allowance	2,000
Claim 80%	1,600
Written down value	8,000

2nd year - 20% allowance	1,600
Claim 80%	1,280
Written down value	6,400

For cars please note that the maximum claim is £3,000. From 6th April 2009 the claim is based on CO_2 emission, and the claim will be either a 20% or a 10% allowance depending on whether the emission is below or above 160 g/km. Interestingly there is no restriction on cars costing over £12,000.

Apart from cars, there is now an annual claim whereby the total of expenditure up to £100,000 can be claimed in any one year. From April 2012 this figure drops down to £25,000.

In the "full" return, you will see 2 columns for expenses - 'total' and 'disallowed'. You put all your expenses in the total column, and the 20%'s of motor and telephone costs (or other proportion), plus the unclaimed fraction of home expenses, in the 'disallowed' column. Further down the section you will see where to deduct the disallowed amount from the total expenses, producing the claimable figure, and thereby the taxable profit or loss.

If you are working as a partnership, you will need to enter these details into a partnership tax return, in which you also are required to state the split of the profit or loss. Here - unless the Revenue think you are blatantly misrepresenting the facts purely to gain a tax advantage - the Tax Inspector will accept the statement of split results to be acceptable to both parties, although the return will only be signed by one of them. The respective shares are then transferred to individual sections in each partner's own tax return called 'Partnership Short'.

This is certainly where you should give thought to the allocation bearing in mind the actual division of the workload, but also having regard to the tax implications where one partner already has other income. You should really seek advice particularly if you are looking to split early year losses, with potential tax repayment claims going back over three years. In this regard be aware of the tax regulation, introduced in February 2004 and now re-emphasised, stating that for a partner to be able to claim full loss relief he or she must be working in the business for at least 10 hours per week.

To calculate any resultant tax bill, you will get a set of tables with your tax return, which look complicated but actually do the job, or you can refer to tables in this book from which you can see a less complicated method. If you are working out a tax repayment following a loss, then basically what you are doing is re-computing total income including earnings from other sources including your 'day job', working out the tax bill on this smaller amount due to including the loss, calculating an adjusted tax bill, comparing this with tax already paid under PAYE (usually), and claiming back the difference. I include a formula later for you to follow.

Don't get into hot water -

get your VAT returns

in on time!

Chapter 10

VAT Returns

Registration is currently compulsory when annual turnover reaches £73,000. Definitions of turnover may vary between businesses, for example it can be expressed as "total sales" in many cases, "commission income" in others, or "commission plus personal (not group) sales" for direct selling businesses. If necessary agree a definition with HMRC.

Voluntary registration can be agreed by HMRC at an earlier stage, and they will also accept a request to tie in the quarterly accounting dates to the business year end which makes for easier reporting.

The first quarter may actually only be for one or two months, depending on the date of registration, but thereafter the returns will follow quarterly with a month's grace to submit the return with an appropriate cheque or of course claim a refund. You can now file and pay VAT online.

The first return often leads to a repayment because, in this return only, you can reclaim any VAT paid on business expenses within a 6 month

Notes Page

period prior to registration - plus 3 years back for capital items still used in the business. Similar rules do not apply to income, so there can be a one-off cash flow bonus here. Make sure you claim it, simply by inflating the figures on the first VAT return in the appropriate boxes.

VAT returns are simple forms, recording the VAT on sales (outputs), deducting VAT on purchases (inputs) and accounting for the difference. You separately record the 'net' (without VAT) sales and purchases on the same form.

It is important to get the returns in on time, as you can incur penalties and interest for being consistently late.

For businesses whose taxable turnover is less than £150,000 p.a. there is now an alternative method for dealing with VAT known as the "flat rate scheme". Here, instead of preparing a standard rate return as above, you ignore expenditure and apply a prescribed percentage to your income based on HMRC tables according to your particular trade sector. By grossing up your income at the current VAT rate, and then paying over the designated percentage of this figure, no further calculations are necessary.

Notes Page

This method is advantageous particularly where only commission income is received and where little VAT on expenditure could be claimed.

It is important to seek professional advice before choosing the flat rate basis to ensure it is in your best interest. In preparing annual accounts you include as income the grossed up receipts, and amongst expenditure you include the amounts of VAT actually paid over to HMRC as well as the VAT element of all expenses.

Notes Page

Chapter 11

Self-employed Tax Planning

In this chapter I just want to mention the areas where advice should be sought in order to minimise tax liabilities or maximise tax refunds as can happen in the early years of a new business. I leave it to the readers to make their own detailed enquiries, this book is not appropriate for that purpose, but let me at least point you in the right direction! All of this is in addition to ensuring that you are claiming all available business expenses and allowances.

New Businesses

Quite generous regulations apply here because section 72 of the 2007 Income Tax Act allows for the carry back of trading losses incurred during the first 4 years of a new business against taxed income in the previous 3 years. For example if 2010/11 was your first trading year, you could look back to the tax year 2007/08 and then come forwards to find any taxed income to offset against the loss, and thereby recover some of the tax. You can always do this on a current year basis, but if for instance you gave up employment to start your new business, you can use this section 72 tax refund opportunity for up to the first 4 years – one necessary test will be to satisfy your inspector that your new business is commercially viable and not just a loss making hobby!

It is also perfectly possible to maximise this claim by working as a partnership and using one partner's higher tax rate to increase the refund. This might require the partner receiving the refund to be able to prove at least 10 hours a week in the business.

Limited Companies

Once a taxpayer has reached the high rate tax threshold, then a Limited Company might be a better tax vehicle in which to operate. The downside is more formality and therefore cost, the upside can be tax benefits from receiving remuneration as small salary and dividend which to the individual can be tax and NI free.

Directors Loan Account

If, as above, you move your business from sole trader or partnership into a Limited Company, you can in effect sell it to the company. This would require an arm's length valuation based on average profits etc, and then in the company's books you would create a goodwill amount on the one side, and a loan account on the other as presumably a new company would not have the funds to pay. There would be a personal capital gains liability on the valuation – currently using the entrepreneurial relief this would only be 10% - but you would be creating a loan which could be withdrawn tax-free in the future…..assuming funds were available!

VAT

If it would help to avoid VAT registration due to having to aggregate 2 or more turnovers of separate self-employed businesses, then by turning one into a Limited Company or a partnership which you do not control, the aggregation principle would not apply and each would have to reach the VAT annual turnover threshold, currently £73,000, before registration became obligatory. This would be most useful if your customers were private e.g. hairdressing, and could not recover VAT themselves – an extra 20% might put them off, or by absorbing this yourself you would earn less profit.

Notes Page

Chapter 12

Payment of Tax

Tax is paid twice a year, January 31st and July 31st following the submission of the self-assessment tax return by January 31st. This will also include any Class 4 national insurance contributions due (see tables).

Paying tax is further complicated if your initial payment of tax exceeds £1,000. If this is the case, then when paying the due amount on 31 January you will have to add 50% on account of the next tax year, based on the assumption that the profits will at least be the same. This same procedure also applies to the July instalment so when it comes to the following January you will only have a balance to pay if profits have increased, plus a repeat payment on account for the next year. Thereafter with the same principle applying (and only a balance being paid in January for the previous year) you are really paying in advance of the current year end. Apart from the £1,000 limit, the only other way to avoid this is to claim that the current year's results are going to be worse than the previous one, or that other income (such as a salary) has now ceased and so the overall tax bill will fall.

Interest is charged for late payments, penalties for no payments at all, and surcharges can be applied for long delays. Surcharges do not apply to payments on account, although these can attract interest if paid late.

To avoid penalties & surcharges

make sure you pay any

tax due on time

Chapter 13

Key Dates

The dates here follow the fiscal year starting with 6th April 2011. For subsequent years simply move all the dates forward.

6th April 2011
New tax returns for 2010/11 sent out.

31st July 2011
Second instalment of tax for 2010/11 is due if you are liable.

31st August 2011
A further 5% surcharge for any tax still unpaid for 2009/10.

31st October 2011
Your tax return must be submitted if you want the HMRC to calculate the tax due. This is also the last day for filing the paper tax returns for 2010/11.

31st January 2012
This is the last day for online filing for the 2010/11 returns. The balance payment for 2010/11 is due, as well as the first instalment for 2011/12.

28th February 2012

A 5% subcharge will be added to any tax still unpaid for 2010/11.

6th April 2012

New tax returns for 2011/2012 send out.

Key dates to remember

Chapter 14

Taxpayers Claiming Benefits

There are many people who become self-employed while claiming state benefits. It is important that the relevant benefit paying body is made aware of the business. However, it does not necessarily mean that the benefits being claimed will be lost or reduced.

State benefits can generally be split between those that are means tested and those that are not. The means tested benefits needs to take the business into account when calculating the benefit payment. The business is merely another source of income. It is the measure of that income and possibly the hours worked that are relevant.

Quite often the initial trading period will incur a tax loss due to the marketing costs exceeding income whilst you are trying to build the business. The tax loss will reduce your income for benefit purposes and can increase the benefit payments, or at the least ensure they continue unchanged.

Jobseeker's Allowance

JSA is generally paid to people who are seeking full time work. Being self-employed does not necessarily stop the benefit, provided you are still in a position to take a full time job. This is because the business in the initial stages may well be run on a part-time basis (evenings and weekends).

Carer's Allowance

This may be affected by the business. As a carer you are required to be able to provide care for at least 35 hours per week and there is an income limit.

Incapacity Benefit

It is possible to claim incapacity benefit whilst running a work from home business. However, there are some complex rules about working hours and earnings.

Income Support

This is a benefit paid to people with low income. Therefore, the initial period when the business is developing and not making profit will not affect the claim. However, the DWP will expect evidence to show the lack of income.

Tax Credits

This is a means tested state benefit and nothing to do with tax. The Revenue rather than the DWP were given the job of running the TC system. TCs unlike other benefits are based on the tax year. Any change in personal circumstances or income needs to be notified to the TC Office as soon as possible to ensure that the system pays you the correct amount. If the business is anticipated to make a loss, then estimating a nil income figure will not change the TC award. But once the actual loss figure is known, it can be used to reduce the overall family income, which may well increase the TC award. It is only when the business is expected to make a profit that you need to carefully consider the estimated profit figure that you give to the TC Office.

Housing Benefit

If you pay rent on your home, it is possible to claim Housing Benefit to help where your income is low. The claim of HB is made to your local authority. The claim is means tested so the business accounts are important. The local authority can ask to see the invoices and receipts, or ask for more information about the accounts. Your savings are also taking into account. If they are more than £16,000 usually no HB will be paid. The savings do not count in the calculation for HB if they are less than £6,000.

The Future

The new coalition government has just announced its intention to simplify the whole arena of benefit claims, but this is not going to happen overnight! We wait to see more details and a timetable in due course.

"I DREAMED LAST NIGHT THAT THE ANIMAL RIGHTS PEOPLE ARE GETTING US FAMILY ALLOWANCES!"

Chapter 15

Tax Rates & Examples

Tax Rates		
	2011/12	**2010/11**
First band of savings income @ 10%	£2,560	£2,440
Base rate band @ 20%	£35,000	£37,400
Higher rate @ 40% on	£35,001 - £150,000	£37,401 and over
Additional rate @ 50% on	£150,001 and over	£150,001 and over

Tax Allowances	**2011/12**	**2010/11**
Personal (under 65)	£7,475	£6,475
Personal (over 65) *	£9,940	£9,490
Personal (over 75) *	£10,090	£9,640
* These allowances reduce where the income is above the income limit by £1 for every £2 of the excess. However they will never fall below the basic allowance.		

National Insurance - Self-Employed Rates	2011/12	2010/11
Class 2	£2.50 p.w.	£2.40 p.w.
Small earnings exception	£5,315 p.a.	£5,075 p.a.
Class 4 9%/8% on profits between	£7,225 and £42,475	£5,715 and £43,875
+ 2%/1% on profits over	£42,475	£43,875

Example - Income Tax Calculation 2010/11

	Gross Income (say)		Tax Deducted (say)
Salary, P60	10,000		1,000
Private Pension	2,000		400
Self-employed Profit	5,000		0
	17,000		£1,400
Personal Allowance	6,475		
Taxable	£10,525		
	£10,525	@ 20%	£2,105
Tax Paid So Far			£1,400
Tax Now Due			£705

Example - Income Tax Repayment Claim 2010/11

	Gross Income (say)	Tax Deducted (say)
Salary, P60	10,000	1,000
Private Pension	2,000	400
Self-employed Loss	(5,000)	0
	7,000	1,400
Personal Allowance	6,475	
Taxable	£525	
Tax to Pay	£525 @ 20%	£105
Tax Paid So Far		£1,400
Tax Refund		£1,295

Chapter 16

Cashflow Projection

CASHFLOW PROJECTION

INCOMINGS

INCOMINGS	JAN	FEB	MAR	APR	MAY	JUN	JUL	AUG	SEP	OCT	NOV	DEC
RETAIL SALES												
WHOLESALE SALES												
FEES												
COMMISSION												
RENT												
INTEREST												
CAPITAL INTRODUCED												
TOTAL INCOME												

OUTGOINGS

CASHFLOW PROJECTION

OUTGOINGS	JAN	FEB	MAR	APR	MAY	JUN	JUL	AUG	SEP	OCT	NOV	DEC
COST OF SALES												
PERSONNEL												
PREMISES												
MOTOR & TRAVEL												
ADMINISTRATION												
SELLING												
FINANCE												
CAPITAL												
DRAWINGS												
TOTAL EXPENDITURE												

Note: These are only the group headings. Either on the same schedule, or a back-up one, you'll need to set out the detailed expenditure behind each category.

102

CASHFLOW PROJECTION - SUMMARY

CASHFLOW PROJECTION - SUMMARY

	JAN	FEB	MAR	APR	MAY	JUN	JUL	AUG	SEP	OCT	NOV	DEC
BALANCE AT START												
INCOMINGS IN MONTH												
OUTGOINGS IN MONTH	( )	( )	( )	( )	( )	( )	( )	( )	( )	( )	( )	( )
BALANCE AT END												

The idea of this summary schedule is to plot how cash flow moves up or down during the year, and how it ends up at the end.

Starting with an opening bank balance on 1st January, add incomings, deduct outgoings and reach a new balance. Then record this as the opening balance in February and repeat the exercise throughout the rest of the year, ending up with an estimated bank balance at 31st December.

The purpose behind a cash flow is to see how much extra funding a business will need based on the highest overdraft reached during the year.

For personal advice on all tax matters
contact us at

DSL Accounting Ltd.
Botanical House, 15 Guy's Cliffe Road,
Leamington Spa
Warwickshire CV32 5BZ
Tel: 01926 422872
Fax: 01926 435211
www.dslaccounting.co.uk

Notes Page

Notes Page

Notes Page

Notes Page

Notes Page

Notes Page

Notes Page

Notes Page